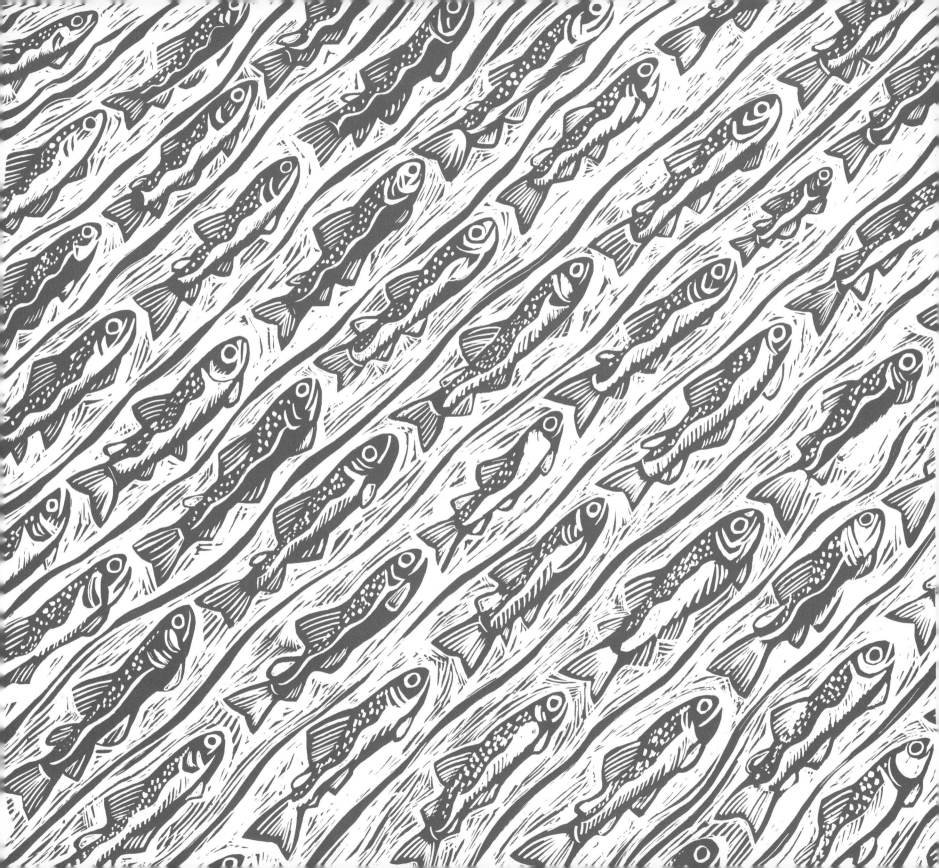

CREEKFINDING

A True Story

JACQUELINE BRIGGS MARTIN

ILLUSTRATIONS BY CLAUDIA McGEHEE

University of Minnesota Press
Minneapolis • London

THE CREEKFINDING MACHINE

An excavator is a machine
that chomps dirt.
Excavators dig holes for basements,
trenches for water pipes, paths for roads.

Sometimes excavators help find lost creeks.
How do they do that?

How does a creek get lost?
Especially a creek that started long ago,
  with a spring that burbled out of the ground
    and tumbled itself across a prairie valley.

The creek wasn't just water.
Insects whirred in and around the creek.

Brook trout grew fat in the creek,
lunching on insects.
Frogs chirupped by the creek,
ready for their buggy share.
Birds watched at the streamside,
hungry for bugs, fish, or frogs.

The insects—stoneflies, dragonflies, caddisflies—

The frogs—spring peepers, leopard frogs, pickerel frogs, green frogs

Well, the creek did not lose itself.
A farmer used a bulldozer
to stuff the creek with dirt
so he would have more
space to grow corn.

He channeled the water from the spring into a ditch at the edge of the field.

No water—
no water bugs, no frogs,
no birds,
and no brook trout.

The lost creek was quiet under the sun.

TROUT IN A CORNFIELD

Years later, a man named Mike
bought that field and the hillside.
Mike wanted to grow a prairie in
    the old cornfield,
to partner with the sun and soil,
    grow tall grasses and flowers.

One day, as Mike was out working,
a neighbor came by and said that long ago
he had caught a brook trout in that very spot.
A brook trout in a cornfield? No way!

PARTNERING WITH THE CREEK

Mike knew there must have been a creek on that prairie.
He wanted to find the creek,
make a place for brook trout, birds, bugs, and frogs.
He said he would call it Brook Creek.
Others laughed,
said Mike's plan was foolishness.
Lost is lost.

But someone gave him an old photograph,
and he marked the creek's path.
Then he called his friends who owned
big machines.

SCRAPING AND DIGGING

For five days, a bulldozer scraped,
an excavator bit into the ground,
carved holes, dug curves and runs,
tamped rocks for the creek bottom.

The excavator had found the old stream.
Would water fill the path?

Mike said the water remembered.
It seeped in from the sides,
    raced down the riffles and runs,
        burbled into holes, filled the creek.

But a creek isn't just water.
It's plants, rocks, bugs, fish, and birds.

Mike and his friends tucked cordgrass
and other green shoots into the creekbanks.
Three summers grasses grew.
When the creek bed needed more rocks
Mike had a problem.

Heavy trucks crossing
to the creek would press
deep ruts into the ground,
kill new prairie plants.
How could he get more
rocks to the creek?

Small rocks protect the soil under the streambed and are home to many tiny plants and creatures.

Mike waited until winter.
When the ground was frozen hard
cement trucks lumbered across the prairie,
emptied their rocks into the creek,
and left no ruts.

Why not use dump trucks to haul rocks?

Mike didn't want to just dump the rocks in the creek. Cement trucks have chutes so he could put the rocks exactly where the creek needed them.

Rocks settled in.
Plants grew.
Insects flew in,
whirred and buzzed
and laid eggs in the water
    and on the grasses.

After two more years,
small fish called sculpin
swam into the creek.
And that was good news:
sculpin survive only
    in clean, clear water,
the same kind of water that
    brook trout need.

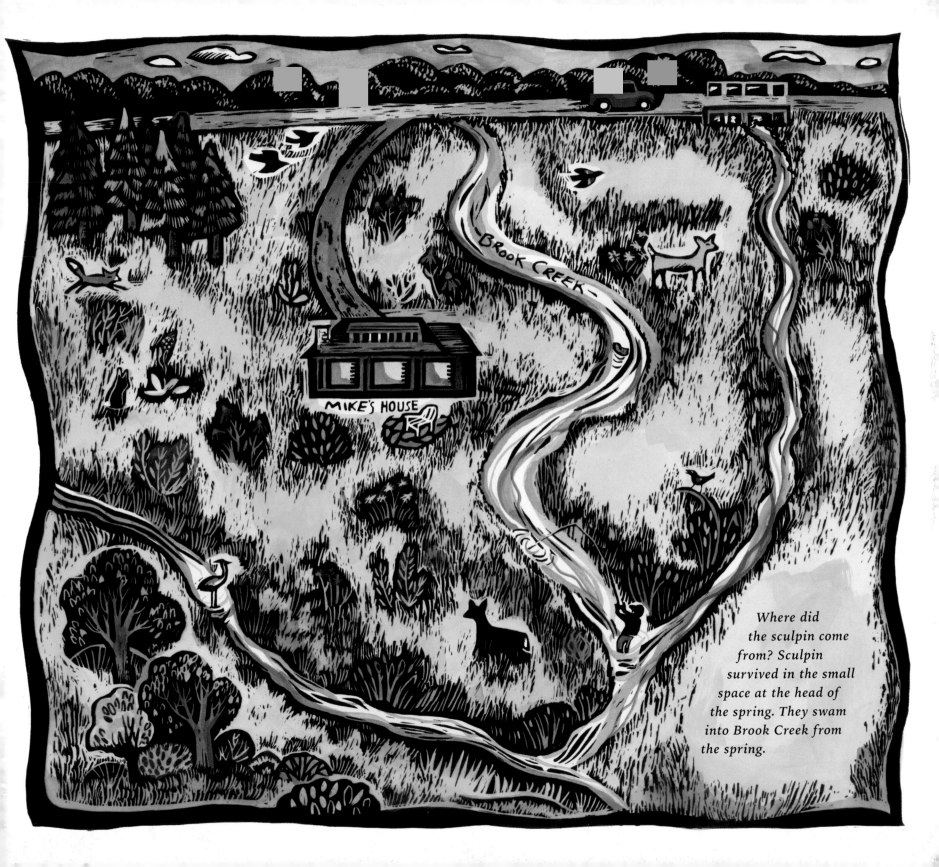

BROOK CREEK

MIKE'S HOUSE

Where did the sculpin come from? Sculpin survived in the small space at the head of the spring. They swam into Brook Creek from the spring.

TIME FOR TROUT

A pickup truck carried the tub
that held the trout.
Mike and his friends laughed in the morning air,
lugged and dumped buckets of finger-sized fish.
Perhaps Brook Creek laughed, too—tickled by trout.

Because the creek water comes from the ground the temperature stays about the same all year and feels warm in winter, cool in summer —just what the trout babies need.

Water was right. Food was right.
Trout snapped up bugs and grew for two summers.
In the second fall, the rocks proved perfect places for the fish to lay eggs.

Brook trout change color during egg-laying season, becoming bright red and orange.

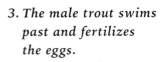

1. The female trout uses tail fins to scoop out a bowl—a redd—in the gravelly creek bottom.

2. She releases 15–60 pea-sized eggs.

3. The male trout swims past and fertilizes the eggs.

4. The female uses her fin to cover the eggs with gravel and swims on to make another redd.

Winter came . . .

Would the eggs survive?
Snowstorm,
    ice storm,
        cold wind ...

FISH SQUIGGLES

Then, one late winter morning—
fish squiggles, no longer than a thumbnail!

Squiggles grew into fat trout,
    who laid eggs in turn
        to hatch more generations of trout
at home in Brook Creek.

MAYBE A CHUCKLE, MAYBE A THANKS

If you went to the creek with Mike,
you'd see the water.

But a creek isn't just water.
You'd see brook trout and sculpin.
You'd hear the outdoor orchestra—
  herons, snipe,
    bluebirds, yellowthroat warblers;

How did the birds find the creek? Mike thinks they found it while looking for new food.

frogs, returned home;
and insects—
thousands, and thousands,
and thousands of insects.

How did the frogs find the creek? Frogs explore during rains, and perhaps they found Brook Creek on one of their wet wanderings.

You'd hear the water ripple and burble—maybe a chuckle—
    maybe a thanks—

to Mike and the big machines that found the creek.

AUTHOR'S NOTE

I have always been drawn to stories of finding and fixing, stories of patching what has been broken. And that is what really happened to Brook Creek. It had been buried under piles of soil. Lost.

Mike found the creek and fixed it with big machines, plants, rocks, and gravel. Then came the bugs, birds, frogs, and fish. Finally Mike added the brook trout. This little creek is now home to a huge world of blooming, buzzing, chirping, and swimming—as it had been for thousands of years. Mike made this one place whole again. And that is why I love this story.

ILLUSTRATOR'S NOTE

One hot July afternoon, I visited Prairie Song Farm, home to Brook Creek, to gather images and impressions for this book's illustrations. As I waded into the deep greenness, all sorts of creatures—winged, scaled, feathered, and furred—bustled in the grasses and along the water banks. I wanted to re-create the textures and colors I saw, so readers could "walk" alongside Brook Creek as they learned about its restoration. I made the ripply, sturdy lines of earth, water, and sky in scratchboard and painted the prairie greens, creek blues, and everything in between with watercolors and dyes.

MORE ABOUT MIKE

Michael Osterholm grew up in northeast Iowa in The Driftless, a region of steep hills and deep valleys never flattened by glaciers, unlike much of the Midwest. He went to college and earned a PhD in public health. He is recognized around the world as an expert on infectious diseases. His work focuses on keeping people healthy: preventing epidemics or illness from contaminated food or bioterrorism. He has received many honors for his efforts.

Mike is passionate about the prairie, cold water streams, brook trout, and partnering with the earth. This is what he says about finding Brook Creek:

As a kid I loved exploring the creeks and caves around my home. As an adult, once I heard there had been a spring-fed creek in that valley, finding it and restoring it became my dream. I believed we could do it. There were a lot of naysayers, but the science part of my brain said if the stream flowed once it could flow again. And the nature-loving part of my brain said wouldn't it be a wonderful gift to bring back these trout that had lived in Iowa for thousands of years? There are now very few places in Iowa where brook trout can survive. I wanted to help make a place where they would be able to thrive for generations to come.

Restoring Brook Creek reminds all of us—kids, too—that dreams do come true and that our dreams make a difference. We can restore parts of our world that have been lost or degraded. I hope kids will remember from this story that we can change the world by acting on our dreams.

For all those who take care of our green places—
by picking up trash, planting flowers, or
finding lost creeks. —J. B. M.

For Callie and Lane, the next generation
of outdoor adventurers. —C. M.

The University of Minnesota Press gratefully acknowledges the generous assistance provided
for the publication of this book by the Margaret W. Harmon Fund.

Published by the University of Minnesota Press
111 Third Avenue South, Suite 290
Minneapolis, MN 55401-2520
http://www.upress.umn.edu

Book design by Brian Donahue / bedesign, inc., and Claudia McGehee

ISBN 978-0-8166-9802-8 (hc)
A Cataloging-in-Publication record for this book is available from the Library of Congress.

Printed in China on acid-free paper
The University of Minnesota is an equal-opportunity educator and employer.

24 23 22 21 20 19 18 17   10 9 8 7 6 5 4 3 2 1

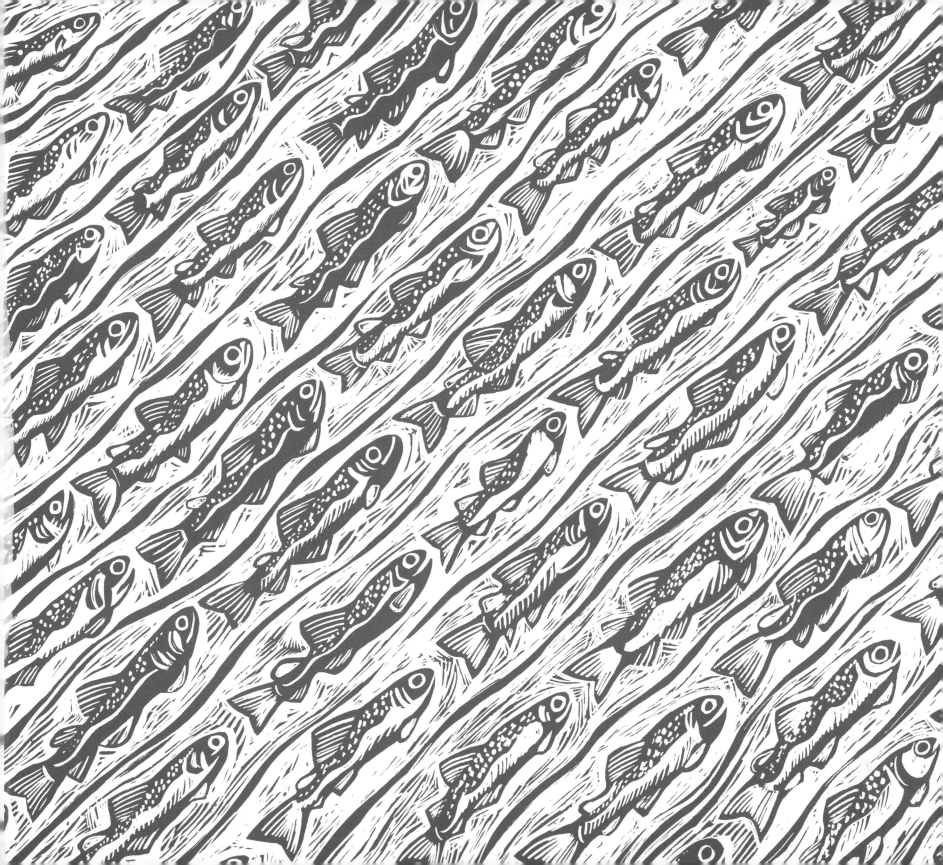